# A wound in time

## Pagan prayers for a modern world

**Lucía Moreno-Velo**
**Gwyneth Box**

© Lucía Moreno-Velo and Gwyneth Box

**Texts:**
Lucía Moreno-Velo & Gwyneth Box

**Photos:**
Lucía Moreno-Velo, pages 2, 11, 52
Rita Moreno-Hoffmann, pages 8, 28
Karine Hoffmann, pages 16, 27, 37, 45, 49, 59

**Book design:**
Tantamount

First published August 2020.

https://modernpaganprayers.com

For those who share the journey.
For those who go on ahead.
And for those we leave behind.

*GEB*


To Karine, for reflecting an image of myself
I can strive to embody. Yes, even after 25 years.
And to Our Lady of Corona, for appearing
to me, in the long tradition of Divinity, in
a dream, larger than life, and downloading
a prayer into my mind.
Thank you.

*LMV*

Morning                                                                               1

   Morning dedication                  3

Our Lady of Corona           5

   A prayer to Our Lady of Corona    6

   A prayer in sickness         9

   Final testament            10

   A blessing for dead bodies, that they may live again    12

   A blessing for departing souls    14

   An incantation to protect my home    17

The Weaver of Worlds         19

   A prayer to the Weaver of Worlds    20

   A prayer for peace while sheltering in place    22

   A blessing on the messengers    24

   A blessing for technology    29

   A blessing for those who break lockdown    30

   A blessing on the ones who walk    32

   A prayer for forgiveness of excess    34

   A prayer to find purpose in lockdown    36

The Horned God         39

   A prayer to the Horned God    40

   A blessing for the cathedrals we destroyed    42

   A blessing on all the creatures    46

   A prayer that our leaders may be guided    50

   A prayer for personal growth    53

Evening         55

   Litany of thanksgiving    56

Morning

## Morning dedication

In the tree outside my window, the birds were singing at dawn;
I, too, raise my voice in thanksgiving.

On the neighbor's stoop, the cat grooms herself, carefully, earnestly;
I wash away the past and start each day anew.

The oranges on my kitchen counter are bright and unashamed;
I will be true to myself in body and mind.

The coffee cuts through early morning blur to clear my head;
I will offer honesty to those I deal with.

There are dandelions in the yard, their faces wide and welcoming;
I greet this day and all it brings with cheerfulness.

# Our Lady of Corona

# A prayer to Our Lady of Corona

Hail, Our Lady of Corona

May your name be called
and your tale be told

You, who hold our breath
and storm our blood
and bid us choose
between life and market

Do not turn my defenses against me
but pass me by

Do not lay your hand upon me
nor touch my loved ones

Do not stop your feet at my door
but spare my home
and that of my neighbors

For I have chosen to live
and to care
and to love

Hail, Our Lady of Corona

May I always have breath
to call your name
and tell your tale

So mote it be ➶

## A prayer in sickness

I call upon you,
body of mine:
be strong

I give you rest;
give me ease

I give you food;
give me strength

I give you water;
give me vigor

I give you care;
give me health

I call upon you,
body of mine:
be well. ๑

## ◇ Final testament

A spark of life
cherished in the waters
of my mother's womb
I was born, gasping, into air
to travel the paths of earth.

When death takes me,
may fire purify my body
and the ashes be cast
to the elements
to drift on the wind
to mix with the rain
and fall gently, again,
to earth. ๑

11 ℓe

## A blessing for dead bodies, that they may live again

Blessed be the bodies
that, having merrily lived,
now part with the soul they held

Feet no longer dancing
hands no longer raised
mouths no longer exploding in outrage
or in laughter

May you melt into rivers
be crushed into soil
fly up in ashes
or in air

That you may be home to souls
that need not life to live

And then
be eaten, drunk and breathed,
digested and metabolized
into thorn, bone or flesh

And merry meet with life again. ᥩ

## A blessing for departing souls

I bless you, departing souls,
releasing the bodies that held you,
no longer bound by matter,
decarnated.

I see you with the eye of consciousness,
spiraling up, up towards the threshold.

Whatever you might find on the other side,
I ask you, do not forget that you were once human,
inhabiting matter that could shiver,
feel pain and desire,
and that you walked the Earth, as I do,
in all its glory and its horror.

I bless you, departing souls,
and wish you the best on your journey.
May you incarnate in flesh, or leaf, or stone,
or not at all, as is your choice.

I bless you, departing souls,
spiraling up, up towards the threshold.

I hope your life was full.
*Bon voyage.* ৶

# An incantation to protect my home

My home is safe and protected.
Strong is my threshold
and only good is welcome.

My home is fresh and clean.
Proud stand my walls
embracing health within.

My home is wealthy and affluent.
My roof is watertight
and harbors only abundance.

My home is happy and calm.
Open are my windows
to peace, love and joy.

My home is safe and protected.
Blessed be my home
and all who dwell here.

# The Weaver of Worlds

# A prayer to the Weaver of Worlds

Beloved Lady
foremost amongst the goddesses
you who are mother, daughter, sister, wife,
who, through your wisdom, teach us
to cherish the past, to accept the present
and to await the future with fortitude

*Oh Lady*
*bless us and protect us*
*grant us patience and hope*

Beloved Lady
you who throw the shuttle on the world's loom
and set the stitches on the ground of our lives
the zigzags, crosses, knots,
the twists and slips

Oh Lady
the familiar fabric is fraying
the colors have faded
and the pattern is lost

*Oh Lady*
*bless us and protect us*
*grant us patience and hope*

Beloved Lady
wind the clouds on your distaff
– the soft cirrus and the thundercloud –
ravel the threads of our consciousness
gather up the wisps of our hopes
and the strands of our prayers

Oh Lady
spin the thread anew
with fresh colors, strong and bright,
weave us a new cloth of life

*Oh Beloved Lady.* ৩

## ◇ A prayer for peace while sheltering in place

May this place where I shelter
be a place of peace

May it harbor compassion
and understanding

May tenderness come nest in it
and friendship make it its home

May it be filled with patience and calm
leaving space only
for companionship, love and fun

May it be a fortress, standing strong
against the outside storm
that trickles in
through news and social media

May it encourage
warmth and loving moments,
hugs and tickles,
respect and communication

May this place of shelter
be a place of peace,
its silence broken only
by conversation
and laughter. ᥬ

# A blessing on the messengers

A blessing on those who, day by day and door-to-door,
drop photocopied notes with names and phone numbers
that offer help and friendship to neighbors and strangers

*A blessing on the messengers*

A blessing on the mailman in his powder-blue shirt and postal-blue shorts
who brings letters from far-off and technologically-challenged
friends and family members and carries our replies to them

*A blessing on the messengers*

May Mercury lend them his winged sandals
that their steps may be light and sure

*A blessing on the messengers*

A blessing on those who drive branded delivery vans
and bring us food and drink and other essentials from the store

*A blessing on the messengers*

A blessing on those who drive their own vehicles or courier vans
crammed high with cardboard boxes bringing bright highlights to our days
with non-essentials, gifts and fancy goods

*A blessing on the messengers*

A blessing on those who drive their own vehicles or ride their own bikes
balancing insulated bags, foil trays and microwavable packages
bringing home-delivery delicacies to add flavor to our days

*A blessing on the messengers*

May Helios lend them the speed of his golden chariot
drawn by fire-darting steeds
and may he keep the roads dry for them

*A blessing on the messengers*

May the Anemoi send favorable winds that they may travel swiftly
and that their sat navs may be accurate and the traffic lights green

And may they find the parking spaces near their destinations empty

*A blessing on the messengers* ෨

27

## A blessing for technology

Blessed be my phone
for it carries the sound of your voice
into my silent home

Blessed be my computer
for it opens a window into your home
from my lonely home

Blessed be social media
for it brings snippets of your day
to brighten my empty home

Blessed be technology
with its strings of ones and zeros
streaming through the air
– invisible ribbons that connect us
no matter the distance. ᏊᏫ

# A blessing for those who break lockdown

I bless all of you
who break lockdown.

I bless you,
for you are selfish.
May you find the courage
to be thoughtful.

I bless you,
for you are angry.
May you find the courage
to be calm.

I bless you,
for you are afraid.
May you find the courage
to trust.

I bless you,
for you are bored.
May you find the courage
to be patient.

I bless you,
for you are protesting.
May you find the courage
to stay strong.

Whoever you are
and whatever your reasons,
I bless all of you
who break lockdown.

May I find the courage
to respect you. ෨

## A blessing on the ones who walk

Blessed be those who set out on foot
to walk their ten thousand steps each day

May the paths they take be smooth
with sunshine to warm them
and dew to lay the dust

May their shoes be comfortable
and may their stride be sure

Although they travel alone
and keep their due distance
may they not be lonely
on their daily journey
but recognize companionship
in all around them

May the breath of those they meet
pass safely in the breeze

May they tread lightly
as the road unfurls before them
inviting them onwards

Wherever their daily walk takes them
may the way be clear

And may they return safe, at last, to their homes. ⟲

## ◇ A prayer for forgiveness of excess

We stockpiled and hoarded
for we were afraid

We binged on comfort foods
for we were anxious

We drank too much alcohol
for we wanted to forget

We skipped the salads, fruit and vegetables
for they were expensive and less freely available

We ate too many ready meals and frozen dinners
for we were lazy and dispirited

We ordered delivery and takeouts
for we missed eating out and deserved a treat

We have punished our bodies
We have lost sight of our self-respect
We have forgotten
to be kind to ourselves

We recognize our weakness
and ask for strength

May we have the courage
to forgive ourselves
and make a new beginning. ෴

# A prayer to find purpose in lockdown

As I stand inside this wound in time
a time outside time
life halted

May I no longer feel the need
to gather words and objects

May I no longer want to please
and be seen or be liked

May I no longer fall prey
to fear or shame or habit

May my life be stripped of ballast
and the chaff and the hay be cast aside
that I may find my Truth, like a needle,
sharp and shining

A purpose I can call my own. ෨

.

The Horned God

## A prayer to the Horned God

Horned God, oh Horned One, heed my call:
tear down, break through the office wall;
send the dolphin and the boar;
push the ivy through my door

*All that is wild, wild and untamed,*
*hear my call and ride again*

Oh Horned One, God of hoof and bone,
engender flower, and quicken thorn;
tear down every wall and fence,
claiming what is yours again

*All that is wild, wild and untamed,*
*hear my call and ride again*

Horned God, I charge you by your name,
ride and dance and sing again;
make us mad with your sweet sound;
raise us up and cast us down

*All that is wild, wild and untamed,*
*hear my call and ride again* ꙮ

# A blessing for the cathedrals we destroyed

Blessed be this cathedral
– the landscapes and the habitats –
with her furnishings, centuries old,
burned down to free up land,
soil eroded into thin air

> *we needed the money*
> *and the corn syrup*

Blessed be this cathedral
– the forests rich with vitality –
with her great living pillars
that we felled and killed

> *we needed the money*
> *and the flat-pack furniture*

Blessed be this cathedral
– the rocks and the mineral world –
that now stands soulless
for we stripped her bare

>	*we needed the money*
>	*and the metal for smartphones*

Blessed be this cathedral
– the seas and the oceans –
that we filled with plastic;
her gargoyles are gone
for they prefer clean buildings

>	*we needed the money*
>	*and a place for our garbage*

Blessed be this cathedral
– our own brothers and sisters –
who we starved to death
overworked for food stamps
put in jail, raped and tortured

*we needed the money,*
*cheap labor and porn*

Blessed be this cathedral
– our beloved Mother Earth –
may she not wait to be rebuilt
but rise from her sickbed
and take us down. ๑

45

## A blessing on all the creatures

*Blessed be those who dwell in the green*
*those who dwell in the dark*
*hearts beating in the in-between*

*May their voices be heard*
*May their beauty be seen*
*May their lives be honored*
*May their souls be revered*

Blessed be those who dart,
those who wriggle, who crawl and creep
Blessed be those who burrow
down, down and deep

Blessed be those who swoop
and those who soar and glide
Blessed be those who dance
and delight in the high blue sky

Blessed be those who dwell in the edgeland
in ocean or sea, in the tundra
in desert, in hedgerow, in wetland
in grassland, in forest or jungle

*Blessed be those who dwell in the green*
*those who dwell in the dark*
*hearts beating in the in-between*

Blessed be those with jewel-bright eyes
with feather, fur and scale
Blessed be the ancient, patient ones
with hoof and horn and tail

Blessed be those dressed in blossom
in leaf, tendril and thorn
Blessed the dark and silent ones
with forms and shapes unknown

*Blessed be those who dwell in the green*
*those who dwell in the dark*
*hearts beating in the in-between*

Blessed be those who dwell among us
in public drains and city parks
unnoticed and invisible
in our gardens and our yards

Blessed be those who share our houses
who enter without keys
Blessed those who make their homes
beneath tiles or under eaves

Blessed be the noiseless ones who watch
from behind the skirting boards
hidden in the cracks and crevices
of our protecting walls

*Blessed be those who dwell in the green*
*those who dwell in the dark*
*hearts beating in the in-between*

*May their voices be heard*
*May their beauty be seen*
*May their lives be honored*
*May their souls be revered* ๏

# ◇ A prayer that our leaders may be guided

At this time of transition, as we stand on the threshold of change
we offer up a prayer for all our leaders and decision makers
for it is in moments such as these that our destiny is shaped.

May the advisors and scientists find the serenity in which to do their jobs
and the clarity to report their conclusions accurately and without bias

May our governments and policy makers listen to the information they receive
and find the wisdom to interpret it correctly and act appropriately

May the opposition politicians put aside party rivalries
and find the magnanimity to act for the greater good

May our business leaders combine the wit to identify the opportunities
with the social conscience to resist acting out of greed and self-interest

May our law enforcement agents find the strength to remain neutral,
and the courage to display fair-mindedness in all their dealings

May our civic leaders find sympathy, tolerance and understanding
to unite and bring their communities together in harmony

May all the carers find peace of mind and the patience
to be kind to those in their charge and to treat them with respect

May each of us be granted personal composure and resilience
that we may act with humanity, honor and kindness at all times

May all of our leaders, private or public, personal or political
recognize the power that they wield due to their office
and may they resist the temptation to abuse their position

At this time of transition, as we stand on the threshold of change
we offer up a prayer for our leaders and decision makers
that their choices and actions may lead us forward together in peace. &

# A prayer for personal growth

As the woodturner crafts the spindle,
stripping the skin from the blank to reveal the form he seeks,
may each revolution of the earth shape and polish me

As the sculptor chisels the rock,
chipping and splitting to reveal the form within,
may life's knocks soothe and smooth my sharp edges

As the painter mixes the pigments
creating new colors that delight the eye,
may I identify my talents and recognize my potential

As the chef blends the ingredients,
testing and tasting, to devise new flavors and dishes,
may I learn the synergies of my personal strengths

As the weaver weaves the cloth,
each thread contributing to the final design,
may I play my part in the pattern of life.

# Evening

## Litany of thanksgiving

I give thanks for my body and mind
and for those who protect them

*I am grateful for all that I have*

I give thanks for the house I sleep in
and for those who share it

*I am grateful for all that I have*

I give thanks for the bonds of family
in blood and in sacrament

*I am grateful for all that I have*

I give thanks for the animals
that keep me company

*I am grateful for all that I have*

I give thanks for the food and drink
that restore and sustain me

*I am grateful for all that I have*

I give thanks for the stores that I shop at
and for the people who work there

*I am grateful for all that I have*

I give thanks for the paths that I follow
on my daily walk

*I am grateful for all that I have*

I give thanks for the green spaces
and for the cityscapes

*I am grateful for all that I have*

I give thanks for the rain
that nourishes this planet and all that live here

*I am grateful for all that I have*

I give thanks for the sunshine
that warms me by day

*I am grateful for all that I have*

I give thanks for the moon and the stars
that light my nights

*I am grateful for all that I have*

I give thanks to the Universe for all its gifts,
yesterday, today and tomorrow

*I am grateful for all that I have*

My prayers

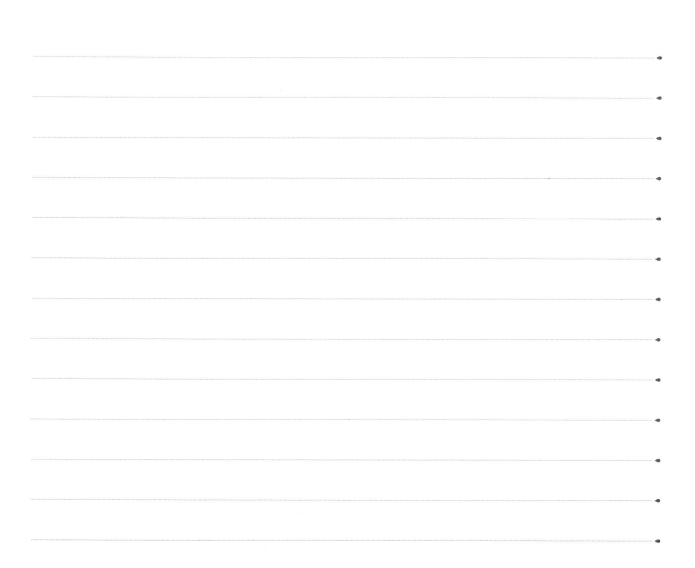

# The authors

## Lucía Moreno-Velo

Lucía is a Pantheist who believes Pagan theology can contribute to the conversation on justice and climate change. She lives with her wife and their two children in Madrid, Spain.

## Gwyneth Box

Spiritually non-tribal, Gwyneth writes in many genres and is an award-winning poet. She leads workshops, mentors non-fiction writers and poets, and appears regularly at open mikes and on the radio.

Printed in Poland
by Amazon Fulfillment
Poland Sp. z o.o., Wrocław